PRAYERSCRIPTS

THE PRAYER OF JABEZ

BLESS ME INDEED

30 Days of Prayers For

UNLOCKING THE OVERFLOW OF
GOD'S FAVOR

CYRIL OPOKU

Published by *Quest Publications*

ISBN: 978-1-988439-81-5

Cover design by *Quest Publications (questpublications@outlook.com)*

Unless otherwise indicated, all Scripture quotations are taken from the World English Bible WEB, which is in the public domain. For more information, visit: www.worldenglish.bible

This book is a work of devotional encouragement. It is not intended to replace biblical study, pastoral counsel, or professional therapy.

Printed in the United States of America.

First Edition: August 2025

For more books like this, visit *PrayerScripts:* https://prayerscripts.org

CONTENTS

PREFACE

"Jabez called on the God of Israel, saying, 'Oh that you would bless me indeed, and enlarge my border! Let your hand be with me, and keep me from evil, that I may not cause pain!' God granted him that which he requested."
—1 Chronicles 4:10 WEB

When I first encountered the prayer of Jabez in Scripture, it felt like a divine invitation to step into more—more of God's blessing, more of His presence, and more of His power at work in my life. Here was a man who, though born under the shadow of pain, dared to believe in the goodness of God. He refused to accept limitation as his destiny, and his simple yet bold prayer shifted the trajectory of his life. That prayer still resounds today as a prophetic key for those who long to see God's undeniable favor shaping their story.

This book, *Bless Me Indeed: Unlocking the Overflow of God's Favor*, is birthed from that same cry. It is not about materialism or chasing after worldly gain. Rather, it is about positioning your heart and your household under the canopy of God's commanded blessing— blessing that silences curses, overturns evil decrees, and establishes your life as a testimony of His covenant faithfulness. Each prayer is Scripture-rooted and Spirit-led, designed to help you pray beyond the ordinary and believe God for the extraordinary.

As you journey through these prophetic prayers, I encourage you to pray boldly, expectantly, and with faith anchored in God's Word. This is not just reading; it is engaging in spiritual warfare, declaring the promises of heaven over your life, and pulling down blessings that belong to you in Christ. May these words stir your spirit, strengthen your faith, and position you to walk in the overflow of divine favor.

I pray that, like Jabez, you will experience the God who hears and answers, the God who turns pain into purpose, and the God who blesses indeed.

Blessed to be a Blessing,
Cyril O. *(Illinois, August 2025)*

How to Use This Book

This book is more than a collection of prayers—it is a spiritual arsenal designed to align your life with the covenant blessings of God. Each prayer is Scripture-based, Spirit-led, and written to help you break free from limitation, overturn curses, and step boldly into the overflow of divine favor. To gain the fullest impact, I encourage you to approach these pages not as passive reading material, but as an active encounter with the living God.

1. Pray with Faith and Expectancy

Every prayer in this book begins with a Scripture. Take time to read the verse slowly and allow it to sink into your spirit. Remember, God's Word is alive and powerful. As you pray, declare the promises boldly, knowing that His Word does not return void. Expect God to respond, just as He granted Jabez what he requested.

2. Make It Personal

These prayers are written in the first person so you can make them your own. Speak them aloud, inserting the names of your family members, your workplace, your church, or your city where applicable. The more you personalize the prayer, the more you will sense its power shaping your reality.

3. Pray Consistently and Persistently

Blessing is often released in layers—like rain that softens the ground until it is saturated. Do not rush through the prayers. Pray them daily, weekly, or as the Spirit leads. Repetition in faith is not vain; it is warfare. Each time you pray, you are reinforcing victory and pushing back the enemy's resistance.

4. Pray with Authority

These are not timid requests; they are bold decrees. Lift your voice as a covenant child of God, covered by the blood of Jesus and backed by heaven's authority. When you pray against curses, delays, and enemies of blessing, do so with confidence that Christ has already won the victory on your behalf.

5. Combine Prayer with Action

As you pray for blessing, also walk in obedience. The blessing of God flourishes where faith and obedience meet. Guard your heart, keep your hands clean, and live in alignment with God's Word. Blessing is not just about what you receive but about how you live under God's covenant covering.

6. Leave Room for the Holy Spirit

These written prayers are a guide, not a limit. As you pray, pause to listen. The Holy Spirit may give you prophetic words, insights, or specific instructions. Follow His lead. Allow Him to expand the prayer, add declarations, or guide you into deeper intercession.

7. Pray with Generational Vision

Jabez's prayer did not stop with him—he sought God's hand and protection so that pain would not be passed down. As you pray these words, see beyond yourself. Pray them over your children, your descendants, and your future generations. Blessing is meant to flow like a river through your lineage.

If you use this book with faith, authority, and consistency, you will discover what Jabez discovered: that God hears the cries of His people and delights to bless them indeed. Let this become your daily practice, your warfare strategy, and your covenant inheritance.

Now, lift your voice, open your heart, and pray: *"Lord, bless me indeed!"*

INTRODUCTION

"Jabez called on the God of Israel, saying, 'Oh that you would bless me indeed, and enlarge my border! Let your hand be with me, and keep me from evil, that I may not cause pain!' God granted him that which he requested."
—1 Chronicles 4:10 WEB

The prayer of Jabez rises from the pages of Scripture like a diamond hidden in the dust of genealogies. In a chapter that lists names and lineages, one man's cry interrupts the ordinary with the extraordinary. His name—Jabez—literally meant "sorrow" or "pain." He was branded from birth with a destiny of hardship, yet he refused to settle for a life limited by that name. Instead, he lifted his voice to the God of Israel with a bold request: *"Bless me indeed."*

This was no casual wish, no shallow plea for comfort. The phrase *"bless me indeed"* in Hebrew carries a sense of intensity, an emphatic doubling—"bless me, bless me!" Jabez was asking not for the ordinary blessing that falls upon all humanity through common grace, but for the distinct, covenantal blessing reserved for the people of God. It was a cry for favor that would break limitations, shatter curses, and mark his life with the unmistakable hand of the Almighty.

The Dimensions of Jabez's Prayer

To understand the depth of Jabez's petition, we must see it against the backdrop of covenant. The God of Israel had revealed Himself as the One who blesses His people. To Abraham, He said: *"I will make you into a great nation. I will bless you and make your name great. You will be a blessing"* (Genesis 12:2). That covenant blessing was not a vague promise—it was specific, covering fruitfulness, protection, inheritance, and generational increase.

Jabez, though born into sorrow, laid hold of that covenant by faith. He understood that his lineage, as part of Israel, was not destined for defeat but for blessing. His prayer shows four dimensions of covenant blessing:

1. **"Bless me indeed"**—Divine favor that overrides curses.

2. **"Enlarge my border"**—Expansion of influence, territory, and opportunity.

3. **"Let Your hand be with me"**—God's presence and power ensuring victory.

4. **"Keep me from evil, that I may not cause pain"**— Deliverance from the enemy's schemes and preservation in righteousness.

Notice the conclusion: *"God granted him that which he requested."* This was not wishful thinking; it was effective prayer rooted in covenant promises. Jabez asked boldly, and God answered abundantly.

The Covenant Promise of Blessing

From Genesis to Revelation, the story of God's people is a story of blessing. Deuteronomy 28 outlines blessings that pursue and overtake the obedient: blessings in the city and in the field, blessings upon family and work, blessings of provision and protection. Psalm 24 describes those who seek God's face as recipients of blessing and righteousness. Isaiah 44 promises an outpouring of the Spirit and blessing upon descendants. The entire witness of Scripture resounds with this truth: God delights to bless His people.

In Christ Jesus, the covenant blessing reaches its fullness. Galatians 3:14 declares: *"that the blessing of Abraham might come on the Gentiles through Christ Jesus, that we might receive the promise of the Spirit through faith."* The blessing Jabez sought is now secured for us through the cross, sealed by the blood, and made effective by the Spirit. What was once a desperate plea has now become a covenant reality.

Walking in the Overflow

This book, *Bless Me Indeed,* is an invitation to step into that overflow. Blessing is not a selfish pursuit; it is a kingdom assignment. God blesses us so that we can be a blessing. The favor He pours out is meant to break the grip of darkness, to silence curses spoken against our families, and to establish us as living testimonies of His goodness.

Each prayer you will encounter in these pages is Scripture-rooted and Spirit-filled. They are not mere words but weapons of warfare, prophetic decrees designed to help you claim what heaven has already released. As you pray them, you are positioning yourself for the blessing that destroys yokes, lifts burdens, and enlarges your destiny.

Beloved, you are not called to live under the shadow of limitation, pain, or defeat. You are called to walk in the blessing of the covenant God—the God who turns curses into blessings because He loves you, the God who enlarges your borders, the God who places His hand upon your life, and the God who delivers you from evil.

May your heart rise in faith as Jabez's did. May your lips declare with boldness, *"Lord, bless me indeed."* And may your life become a testimony of answered prayer, overflowing with the undeniable goodness of God.

DAY 1

BLESS ME INDEED

"Jabez called on the God of Israel, saying, "Oh that you would bless me indeed, and enlarge my border! Let your hand be with me, and keep me from evil, that I may not cause pain.""
—1 Chronicles 4:10 WEB

O Lord, the God of covenant and promise, I rise before You today with a cry that pierces through the heavens: Bless me indeed! Not with the shallow measures of men, not with fleeting treasures, but with the fullness of Your divine favor. Let the oil of Your abundance overflow upon my head until every barren place in my life bursts forth with life. By the blood of Jesus, I silence every voice of limitation, lack, and curse that has warred against my destiny.

Father, I declare that my household and I are no longer confined to narrow places. Where the enemy tried to reduce me, You are expanding me. Where he sought to shut doors, You are opening gates of influence and prosperity. I decree that my portion shall not be stolen by the wicked, nor diverted into the hands of my enemies. By Your strong right hand, lift me out of every valley of scarcity and set me upon the mountain of divine overflow.

Mighty God, let the evidence of Your blessing mark me so distinctly that those who rise against me will stumble and fall in shame. Let Your goodness dismantle the weapons of the adversary, frustrate the counsel of darkness, and rebuke every power assigned to afflict my peace. May Your glory surround me like a wall of fire, and may my life testify that You are the God who blesses beyond measure.

I stand under the canopy of Your blessing and decree that everything connected to me—my family, my work, my health, my ministry—shall blossom and prosper. The heavens are opened over me, and I walk in the inheritance secured by Christ. Let the fragrance of Your blessing flow from me to generations yet unborn, that Your name may be exalted forever.

In Jesus' name, Amen.

DAY 2

I WILL NOT LET GO

"He said, 'Let me go, for the day breaks.' Jacob said, 'I won't
let you go, unless you bless me.'"
—Genesis 32:26 WEB

Ancient of Days, I take hold of You as Jacob did, clinging to the hem
of Your garment with holy desperation. I refuse to release my grip
until the blessing You have ordained for me and my family is fully
released. I am not satisfied with partial breakthroughs or temporary
victories; I contend for the complete inheritance of covenant
blessing that the blood of Jesus has secured.

Every spiritual adversary seeking to deny me this inheritance is
defeated. I break every curse of delay, diversion, and denial in the
name of Jesus. No stronghold of darkness, no generational
bondage, no demonic resistance shall withstand the force of my
faith and the power of Your promise. Lord, I declare that as Jacob
became Israel, my name, my identity, and my destiny are
transformed today.

O God of Abraham, Isaac, and Jacob, let the dew of heaven drench
my life with favor. Release blessings that overthrow the plans of my
enemies, blessings that cover my family in safety, blessings that
establish us as a testimony of Your glory. I declare that my life will
never again be defined by struggle, but by victory and abundance
in You.

I will not be moved by the threats of the enemy. Like a warrior holding fast to his weapon, I cling to You, O God, for You are my shield and my exceedingly great reward. Let every enemy of my soul bow, let every power of darkness flee, and let every mountain of impossibility dissolve before the fire of Your blessing.

In Jesus' name, Amen.

DAY 3

THE BLESSING BRINGS INCREASE

"May God be merciful to us, bless us, and cause his face to shine on us. ... The earth has yielded its increase. God, even our own God, will bless us. God will bless us. All the ends of the earth shall fear him."
—Psalms 67:1, 6-7 WEB

Merciful Father, shine the radiance of Your face upon me and my household. Let Your blessing descend like rain upon thirsty ground, causing every seed we have sown in tears to spring forth with joy. The earth will yield its increase for me, for I am blessed of the Lord. My storehouses will overflow, my health will flourish, my peace will abound, and my generations will bask in Your favor.

Lord, I decree that no spirit of barrenness or stagnation will withstand the power of Your blessing. The works of my hands will not wither in drought, nor will the enemy consume the fruit of my labor. Every demonic embargo that has limited my increase is shattered now. I walk in supernatural productivity, and the land beneath me must respond with abundance.

Father, I call forth blessings that provoke the fear of the Lord in the nations. Let my testimony resound as a beacon of Your glory. Cause the wicked to see the evidence of Your hand upon me and tremble. May every scheme of the adversary against my increase be reduced to dust, for the Lord Himself has commanded the blessing.

I declare that as the earth yields its increase, my family will live under open heavens. Blessings will overtake us, favor will surround us, and goodness will pursue us all the days of our lives. The name of the Lord will be exalted through the fruitfulness You have ordained for us.

In Jesus' name, Amen.

DAY 5

THE BLESSING OF HIS NAME

"Speak to Aaron and to his sons, saying, 'This is how you
shall bless the children of Israel. You shall tell them,
"Yahweh bless you, and keep you. Yahweh make his face
to shine on you, and be gracious to you. Yahweh lift up his
face toward you, and give you peace." So they shall put my
name on the children of Israel; and I will bless them.'"
—Numbers 6:23-27 WEB

Heavenly Father, covenant-keeping God, I stand under the priestly
blessing You commanded for Your people. I declare that Your name
is written upon me and my household. Let Your blessing descend
like fire from heaven, consuming every trace of curse, oppression,
and affliction. Lord, bless me and keep me—preserve my life, shield
my family, and secure our destiny in the shelter of Your wings.

Shine upon me, O God, with the brilliance of Your face. Let every
shadow of darkness around my life be dispelled by the radiance of
Your glory. Pour out grace upon me in overflowing measure,
breaking every chain of guilt, shame, and reproach. Where the
enemy has accused, let Your mercy speak louder.

Lift up Your countenance upon me, Lord, and let peace flood every
corner of my being. I decree that the name of Yahweh is upon me
as a seal of ownership. The devourer cannot touch what is marked
by Your name. The destroyer cannot harm what is sealed by Your

covenant. By this blessing, every evil word spoken against me is nullified, and every curse uttered in secret is destroyed.

Father, I stand in the assurance that when Your name is placed upon me, blessing becomes irreversible. I declare that my family and I live under the perpetual rain of Your favor. Nations will see the mark of Your name upon us and know that we are Yours. Let this blessing establish us as vessels of Your glory in the earth.

In Jesus' name, Amen.

DAY 6

OVERFLOWING BLESSING

"May Yahweh bless you out of Zion, even he who made
heaven and earth."
— Psalms 134:3 WEB

O God of Zion, the Maker of heaven and earth, I lift my voice in
prophetic agreement with Your eternal decree over my life. You are
the Fountain of all blessings, and from Your holy mountain flows
rivers of favor that no enemy can block. I stand in the authority of
Your Word, declaring that every curse, limitation, and resistance set
against my household is overturned by the might of Your blessing.

Let Your blessing descend like rain upon me, saturating my life with
fruitfulness. From the heights of Zion, let divine abundance flood
my family, my labor, my health, and my destiny. Every wicked spirit
that has risen to dry my wells, scatter my seed, or wither my harvest
is shattered by the power of Your throne. No power of hell can
withstand the decree of the Creator who spoke the heavens and
earth into being.

Father, I declare that I am not walking in dryness or scarcity, but in
the overflow of heaven's resources. Your blessing uproots poverty,
cancels barrenness, and destroys the oppression of the enemy.
Angels of blessing, go forth and release into my hands all that
belongs to me by covenant right.

Let Zion's blessing speak louder than the curses of men. Let the
heavens release what belongs to me, and let the earth yield her

increase. By the authority of the Lord of Hosts, I am untouchable by the powers of darkness, for the blessing of Zion clothes me with fire.

In Jesus' name, Amen.

DAY 7

BLESSING UPON MY FAMILY

"May Yahweh bless you out of Zion; and may you see the good of Jerusalem all the days of your life."
— Psalms 128:5 WEB

Father of glory, the Keeper of generations, I decree today that my household is covered under Your eternal blessing. Out of Zion, let the flow of goodness break every chain of evil projected against my family. Where the enemy has plotted destruction, let the blessing of God cancel and reverse it.

I call forth divine favor upon my bloodline. Let every spirit of lack, infirmity, and sorrow that has troubled my family line be consumed by the fire of Zion's blessing. I decree longevity, peace, and joy upon my children and my children's children. No curse of premature death, no bondage of delay, no manipulation of darkness shall prevail, for the goodness of Jerusalem rests upon us all the days of our lives.

Lord, plant my family like olive trees around the table of Your abundance. May our heritage be marked by righteousness, prosperity, and divine preservation. From this day forward, let every altar of wickedness that has spoken against my family scatter in the name of Jesus. Let Your blessing silence every evil voice.

I will see goodness, not evil; joy, not sorrow; life, not death. My eyes will behold the flourishing of my family and the triumph of righteousness in our lineage. Out of Zion, let perpetual blessings locate us, keep us, and elevate us.

In Jesus' name, Amen.

DAY 8

THE WEALTH OF HEAVEN

"Yahweh's blessing brings wealth, and he adds no trouble to it."
— Proverbs 10:22 WEB

Mighty God, the Giver of wealth and the Breaker of curses, I rise today in prophetic declaration that the blessing of the Lord rests upon me. Every wealth that is laced with sorrow from the enemy is rejected. Only heaven's pure blessing will define my life.

I decree that my hands are anointed for productivity, and my labor is fruitful without affliction. I reject the sweat and pain imposed by the enemy, for Your Word declares that Your blessing makes rich without adding trouble. Every power that seeks to tie my prosperity to bondage, pain, or oppression is destroyed by fire.

Father, release over me the treasures of heaven and the hidden riches of the earth. I decree that I am a carrier of kingdom wealth, ordained to advance Your purpose and to break the chains of poverty in my generation. No evil hand will siphon what You have given to me. No dark force will tamper with my inheritance.

From this day, I walk in unshakable abundance. I decree joy-filled prosperity, resources that multiply without sorrow, and blessings that extend to my children. I am marked by divine favor, preserved from the traps of the wicked, and empowered to flourish without limitation.

In Jesus' name, Amen.

DAY 9

A BLESSED NAME

"I will make of you a great nation. I will bless you and
make your name great. You will be a blessing."
— Genesis 12:2 WEB

O Covenant-Keeping God, the One who calls things that are not as
though they are, I declare over my life that I am a vessel of greatness
by Your decree. You have marked me for blessing, and I refuse to be
diminished by the hand of the enemy.

Let every curse that has sought to reduce me, silence me, or bury
my name be broken. I am not forgotten, for You have inscribed my
destiny in the palm of Your hands. My name is lifted, established,
and preserved in righteousness. Where the enemy has tried to drag
my name through reproach, let the blessing of the Lord exalt it with
honor.

Father, make me a channel of blessing. Through my life, let many
encounter Your goodness. Let the works of my hands carry an
anointing that breaks yokes. Let my voice become an oracle of
deliverance and my presence an atmosphere of blessing.

By Your decree, I am not ordinary. I am a city set on a hill, shining
for the glory of the Lord. I will be a blessing to nations, a restorer of
families, and a breaker of demonic chains. Let my name be
associated with victory, favor, and generational impact.

In Jesus' name, Amen.

DAY 10

THE BLESSING OF MULTIPLICATION

"Yahweh's angel called to Abraham a second time out of the sky, and said, 'I have sworn by myself, says Yahweh, because you have done this thing, and have not withheld your son, your only son, that I will bless you greatly, and I will multiply your offspring like the stars of the heavens, and like the sand which is on the seashore. Your offspring will possess the gate of his enemies. All the nations of the earth will be blessed by your offspring, because you have obeyed my voice.'"
— Genesis 22:15-18 WEB

O Lord, the God who swore by Himself, the unchangeable One whose word cannot fail, I enter into the covenant blessing released through obedience. Because You are faithful, my seed is blessed, my lineage is multiplied, and my household is secured under divine favor.

Every demonic voice that has spoken barrenness, delay, or destruction over my life is silenced. My seed will flourish like the stars of the heavens. My inheritance will expand like the sand of the seashore. I declare that no weapon formed against my family will prosper, for we possess the gates of our enemies.

Lord, I decree that every gate of limitation, stagnation, and oppression is torn down. I possess the gate of prosperity, the gate of influence, and the gate of generational impact. My offspring will not bow to the enemy, but will rise in authority, carrying the covenant blessing of Abraham into nations.

Father, let my obedience unlock a transgenerational flow of blessings. Let the nations of the earth be blessed because of my seed. Raise through me a lineage of firebrands, prophets, intercessors, leaders, and kingdom builders who will shatter the works of darkness and establish Your glory upon the earth.

In Jesus' name, Amen.

DAY 11

SHOWERS OF BLESSING

"I will make them and the places around my hill a blessing.
I will cause the shower to come down in its season. There
will be showers of blessing. The tree of the field will yield
its fruit, and the earth will yield its increase. They will be
secure in their land. Then they will know that I am
Yahweh, when I have broken the bars of their yoke and
have delivered them out of the hand of those who made
slaves of them. They will no longer be prey to the nations.
The animals of the earth won't devour them, but they will
dwell securely, and no one will make them afraid. I will
raise up to them a plantation for renown, and they will no
more be consumed with famine in the land, and not bear
the shame of the nations any more. They will know that I,
Yahweh, their God, am with them, and that they, the
house of Israel, are my people," says the Lord Yahweh.'"
—Ezekiel 34:26-30 WEB

Mighty Father, Fountain of every blessing, I step into the covenant
of Your promise that declares showers of blessing over my life. Let
every barren place within me and around me drink deeply of Your
rain. Where the enemy has sown dryness, let Your abundance
spring forth. I decree that my life, my family, and my household are
marked by fruitfulness, secured by Your hand, and overshadowed
by Your goodness.

O Lord, break the bars of every yoke laid upon me and my family.
Tear apart the chains that have bound us in cycles of limitation,

lack, and fear. I proclaim that we will no longer be prey to wicked forces, no longer a target of destruction. By Your Word, I rise above the reproach of famine, barrenness, and shame. Let the plantation of renown You promised spring forth in my household—our name shall be associated with favor, with life, with testimony, and with Your glory.

Father, as Your showers descend, let every curse be overturned and every wilderness turned into a watered garden. Cause my hands to prosper, my labor to yield increase, and my household to dwell in safety. I call forth divine security, and I declare that no beast of darkness shall devour what You have planted in us.

Great Shepherd of my soul, You are with me. Let Your abiding presence mark us as Your people forever. May nations see and acknowledge that we belong to You, for Your blessing makes us untouchable and undeniable. I walk in overflow, I rise in renown, and I live under Your showers of blessing.

In Jesus' name, Amen.

DAY 12

BLESS ME, FATHER

Esau said, "Haven't you reserved a blessing for me?"
—Genesis 27:38 WEB

Holy God, my Father of mercy, today I cry out with holy desperation—bless me, O Lord, bless me indeed! Do not withhold from me the portion You have ordained before the foundation of the world. I refuse to walk empty-handed when You have called me to abundance. Where men may limit or deny, I decree that Heaven's storehouses shall open for me and my family.

Father, silence every voice of opposition that would diminish my inheritance. Break every pattern of loss and deprivation designed by the enemy. I refuse to live beneath my covenant rights, for I am redeemed by the blood of Jesus. Let Your blessing rest heavily upon my head, flowing down into my children, saturating every work of my hands.

Lord of all grace, I reject delay, denial, and defeat. May the fragrance of Your favor surround me, opening doors that no man can shut. Where my enemies desire my downfall, let Your blessing elevate me. Where there has been contention, release peace. Where there has been striving, grant supernatural rest and increase.

O God of Abraham, Isaac, and Jacob, establish my lineage in covenant blessing. May the nations know that I am called by Your name and set apart for Your goodness. By Your decree, I am blessed and cannot be cursed, lifted and cannot be cast down, fruitful and cannot be barren.

In Jesus' name, Amen.

DAY 13

THE BLESSING OF FAVOR

From the time that he made him overseer in his house,
and over all that he had, Yahweh blessed the Egyptian's
house for Joseph's sake. Yahweh's blessing was on all that
he had, in the house and in the field.
—Genesis 39:5 WEB

Faithful Father, God of covenant favor, I step into the blessing of
Joseph today. I decree that everything in my hands, whether small
or great, shall carry the mark of Your blessing. Just as Joseph's
presence caused his master's house to prosper, let my presence
bring divine increase wherever I go. Let businesses flourish, homes
thrive, and territories expand because I am there carrying the
anointing of blessing.

Lord of Hosts, overturn every spirit of sabotage and opposition sent
against my household. Let the enemy's schemes collapse before
they are formed. I declare that my family and I are instruments of
blessing, not of curse, vessels of increase, not of reduction. May
every environment we enter shift under the weight of Your favor.

Great King, let the blessing saturate not only my house but also my
field—my workplace, my ministry, my endeavors, and the dreams
You have placed within me. Let divine productivity abound and
supernatural promotion manifest. Just as You lifted Joseph, lift me
above the traps of my enemies, turning their evil into platforms of
glory.

Father, cause the testimony of my life to reveal that it is You who blesses. Let men testify that for my sake, blessings have come into their midst. Establish my name in the book of the blessed, and let every curse against me and my family be nullified by the authority of Christ's blood.

In Jesus' name, Amen.

DAY 14

APPOINTED FOR INCREASE

Laban said to him, "If I have found favor in your eyes, please stay, for I have divined that Yahweh has blessed me for your sake."
—Genesis 30:27 WEB

O Lord my God, Possessor of heaven and earth, I proclaim today that my life carries the fragrance of divine blessing. Wherever I dwell, increase shall follow. Wherever I labor, prosperity shall spring forth. Let the testimony of Jacob rest upon me—that men will recognize that for my sake, their lives are elevated.

Father, clothe me with undeniable favor that cannot be resisted. Destroy every demonic garment of reproach placed upon me and my family. Let Your glory overshadow us so that even adversaries cannot deny that we are chosen and blessed of the Lord.

I decree that the blessing upon my life will provoke unusual opportunities and divine connections. Let those who encounter me be compelled to release what belongs to me, for the blessing commands it. Let no evil hand siphon my harvest. Let no spiritual thief steal the portion ordained for my household.

God of Jacob, let the works of my hands bear witness to Your covenant. Multiply my seed, expand my influence, and establish my family line in abundance. Let my name be associated with increase and divine prosperity, not with struggle or lack.

I walk in the blessing that distinguishes and elevates. I am set apart for overflow, and I decree that the oil of blessing will never run dry in my house.

In Jesus' name, Amen.

DAY 15

OVERFLOWING HOUSEHOLD BLESSING

Yahweh blessed Obed-Edom and all his house. King David was told, "Yahweh has blessed the house of Obed-Edom, and all that belongs to him, because of God's ark." So David went and brought up God's ark from the house of Obed-Edom into David's city with joy.
—2 Samuel 6:11-12 WEB

Lord of Glory, Eternal King, I invite Your presence, symbolized by the ark, to fill my house. Just as You blessed Obed-Edom because Your presence rested upon him, let Your presence dwell richly within my life and my family. Let the atmosphere of blessing saturate every room, every possession, every endeavor connected to me.

Father, I decree that nothing in my household shall remain untouched by Your favor. My children, my spouse, my work, and even the smallest detail of my life shall carry the mark of divine increase. Where others have struggled, I declare ease. Where others have lacked, I declare overflow.

Break the power of every household enemy that seeks to rob my blessing. Every generational curse, every demonic intrusion, every covenant of poverty—I command them broken in the name of Jesus. My family shall not be a dwelling place of sorrow but a habitation of joy, prosperity, and glory.

O God, let the testimony of Obed-Edom become the testimony of my lineage. Cause the nations to see the undeniable evidence of Your blessing upon us. May my house be a signpost of what happens when the ark of Your presence abides with a man.

Father, let our joy overflow and our lives become a witness of Your glory. For as You have blessed Obed-Edom, so You bless me today.

In Jesus' name, Amen.

DAY 16

OPEN THE WINDOWS OF HEAVEN

"Bring the whole tithe into the storehouse, that there may be food in my house, and test me now in this," says Yahweh of Armies, "if I will not open you the windows of heaven, and pour you out a blessing, that there will not be room enough to receive it. I will rebuke the devourer for your sakes, and he shall not destroy the fruits of your ground; neither shall your vine cast its fruit before its time in the field," says Yahweh of Armies. "All nations shall call you blessed, for you will be a delightful land," says Yahweh of Armies.
— Malachi 3:10-12 WEB

Mighty God of abundance, Yahweh of Armies, I stand today beneath the heavens You have commanded to open over my life. I declare that every curse of lack, delay, and devourer assigned against me and my household is broken by Your Word. You have promised overflowing blessing, and I align myself under Your covenant of obedience and surrender.

By the blood of Jesus, I renounce the works of spiritual thieves and destroyers. Every hand of the devourer stretched toward my finances, my health, my family, or my destiny is rebuked by Your power. Father, release divine fruitfulness over the labor of my hands. Let every vine in my field hold strong and bear its harvest in due season. My storehouse shall never be empty; my dwelling shall never be barren.

Let the fragrance of Your blessing rest on my family, so that nations shall look upon us and call us blessed. Make my home a testimony of Your goodness and a living altar of praise. Father, lift me from the ordinary and mark me with the extraordinary favor that overflows and cannot be contained.

As You pour out Your blessing, let it silence the mockery of enemies and shut the mouths of accusers. Let the blessing rebuke poverty, cancel debt, heal wounds, and release prosperity without sorrow. Establish my family as a delightful land where joy, peace, and abundance are our portion forevermore.

In Jesus' name, Amen.

DAY 17

THE FIRSTFRUITS BLESSING

"The first of all the first fruits of every kind, and every offering of every kind, of all your offerings, shall be for the priests. You shall also give to the priests the first of your dough, to cause a blessing to rest on your house."
— Ezekiel 44:30 WEB

Eternal High Priest, I lift up my life, my labor, and my household as a firstfruit offering before You. I surrender the very best of what I am and what I have, not withholding from You, for You are worthy of my first and my best. By this act of covenant alignment, I prophetically decree that the blessing of the Lord shall rest upon my house.

Lord, by Your Word, let every curse of emptiness and insufficiency be broken. I reject the spirit of famine and lack that has sought to sit at my table. I declare that my barns shall be filled, my cupboards shall never run dry, and my hands shall be empowered to prosper. By the blood of the Lamb, I silence every accuser that says my house shall crumble or my family shall scatter.

Father, bless my household with unity, strength, and peace. Cause every member of my family to flourish like fruitful trees planted by rivers of living water. Let no weapon of strife, sickness, or poverty prevail in this dwelling. Let Your priestly blessing rest as a covering on the roof above us, as a shield at our gates, and as fire upon our altar.

I decree that my home shall not only be blessed but shall become a channel of blessing to others. From this place shall flow generosity, kindness, and abundance that brings glory to Your name. Every enemy that rises against my house is consumed by the fire of Your presence, and every curse sent against us is turned into multiplied favor.

In Jesus' name, Amen.

DAY 18

BLESSED IN EVERY WORD

All these are the twelve tribes of Israel, and this is what
their father spoke to them and blessed them. He blessed
everyone according to his blessing.
— Genesis 49:28 WEB

Father of Generations, the God of Abraham, Isaac, and Jacob, I
stand under the covenantal blessing of the lineage of faith. I declare
that every word You have spoken concerning me and my household
shall come to pass. Just as Jacob blessed his sons according to their
destiny, so I call forth the blessings of heaven over every member of
my family.

Lord, I decree that no curse spoken by the enemy shall land upon
us. Every word of death, limitation, or confusion spoken over our
lives is nullified by the superior word of blessing flowing from Your
throne. I release prophetic blessings upon my children, upon my
work, upon my health, and upon the generations to come after me.

Father, let the distinct blessings ordained for each of us find full
expression. Cause us to walk in the uniqueness of our God-given
destinies. Let the spirit of division, comparison, and rivalry be cast
down, and let unity in blessing mark this family line. Every
generational curse of poverty, strife, or disease is overturned, and a
generational blessing of wealth, wisdom, and favor is established.

Lord, magnify Your goodness in such a way that all who see my
family will marvel at the greatness of Your hand. Let our story be

one of covenant triumph, our testimony one of supernatural favor. Cause us to be carriers of legacy blessings that no enemy can steal, erase, or diminish.

In Jesus' name, Amen.

DAY 19

COMMANDED INCREASE

If you say, "What shall we eat the seventh year? Behold, we shall not sow, nor gather in our increase;" then I will command my blessing on you in the sixth year, and it shall bring forth fruit for the three years.
— Leviticus 25:20-21 WEB

Commanding God, the Lord of increase, I receive Your Word of supernatural provision and multiplication. You are the God who does not depend on seasons or circumstances. Even in times when others fear lack, You command a blessing that carries us beyond natural limitation.

Father, I decree that my household shall not be subject to the cycles of scarcity. While others cry "not enough," we shall testify of overflow. The sixth-year blessing is ours—provision that is commanded, abundance that is undeniable, fruitfulness that sustains for years ahead. Every spirit of fear, anxiety, and worry about provision is silenced by the assurance of Your Word.

I declare that the enemy shall not consume my harvest, nor shall the devourer eat what my hands have sown. Instead, my seed shall multiply, my resources shall stretch, and my cup shall overflow. Father, cancel every spiritual embargo on my income, my career, and my future. Establish divine supply lines from unexpected places, and let my household stand as a testimony of Your commanded blessing.

Lord, make me a steward of abundance that blesses others. Even when famine arises in the land, let my family eat to the full and share with those in need. May the commanded blessing speak louder than every curse and silence the taunts of my enemies.

In Jesus' name, Amen.

DAY 20

THE DEW OF BLESSING

Like the dew of Hermon, that comes down on the hills of
Zion; for there Yahweh gives the blessing, even life forever
more.
— Psalms 133:3 WEB

Father of Glory, I lift my hands to You, the Giver of life and blessing.
Let the refreshing dew of Hermon descend upon me and my family.
Just as dew nourishes the earth, let Your Spirit saturate every dry
place in my life. Pour upon us the blessing that cannot be reversed,
the blessing that carries the fragrance of eternal life.

Lord, I decree that disunity, strife, and division have no place in my
home. Every demonic strategy to sow discord and hatred among
my family members is uprooted. I release the oil of unity, the dew
of peace, and the river of love over my household. Father, let us
dwell in harmony so that Your commanded blessing may remain
upon us without hindrance.

I speak life over every dead dream, every sick body, and every weary
soul in my family. By Your Spirit, let there be renewal, restoration,
and refreshing. The dew of heaven is our portion, and the life of
God flows through our home. We shall not wither; we shall flourish
like trees planted in fertile soil.

Father, cause our family to radiate the beauty of unity, the fragrance
of love, and the abundance of peace. Let our house be a reflection
of Zion, where Your blessing dwells and life flows endlessly. May

every enemy who seeks to dry up our joy or divide our bond be scattered, while Your blessing rests upon us forever.

In Jesus' name, Amen.

DAY 21

COMMANDED BLESSING RELEASED

"Yahweh will command the blessing on you in your barns,
and in all that you put your hand to. He will bless you in
the land which Yahweh your God gives you."
—Deuteronomy 28:8 WEB

O Lord of Glory, Commander of Heaven's hosts, I lift my voice today and align myself with Your decree of blessing. You are the One who speaks and it stands firm, who commands and none can reverse. I declare that Your commanded blessing rests upon me, my household, and the work of my hands. Let every effort, every assignment, every plan ordained by You prosper beyond measure under the canopy of Your favor.

Father, silence the voice of every devourer assigned against my labor. Let the fire of Your Spirit consume every curse, every delay, and every hand of wickedness stretched out against my barns, my finances, my opportunities, and my destiny. No demonic embargo shall withstand the word that You have commanded. Your blessing overtakes me and covers my land, establishing me as a testimony of Your goodness.

Lord, I refuse to walk in lack when You have commanded abundance. I refuse to operate in cycles of failure when You have established me for fruitfulness. I decree multiplication, overflow, and the rain of increase upon every seed I sow. My life is the field that the Lord Himself has blessed.

I rise as a light in the land, a carrier of commanded prosperity and grace. Let the fragrance of blessing spread from my household to generations yet unborn. What You bless cannot be cursed, what You increase cannot be diminished. Let the evidence of Your hand mark my life today and forevermore.

In Jesus' name, Amen.

DAY 22

TURNED FROM CURSE TO BLESSING

"Nevertheless Yahweh your God wouldn't listen to Balaam, but Yahweh your God turned the curse into a blessing to you, because Yahweh your God loved you."
—Deuteronomy 23:5 WEB

Almighty Father, Covenant-Keeping God, I exalt You who turns every curse into blessing. Because of Your steadfast love, no weapon of enchantment, no voice of sorcery, no utterance of the wicked can prevail over me or my family. What the enemy meant for destruction, You have already reversed for my upliftment and favor.

Today, I stand in the blood of Jesus and renounce every generational curse, every evil altar, and every word spoken against my destiny. I decree that curses are overturned, hexes are shattered, and dark decrees are nullified. By the power of Your love, O Lord, I am lifted into blessing, honor, and greatness.

Let the blessing of Abraham, Isaac, and Jacob manifest in my household. Let every Balaam assigned to curse me fall into confusion, and let every wicked prophecy be reversed into testimonies of joy. Where they spoke death, release life. Where they declared lack, release abundance. Where they plotted shame, release honor.

Father, surround me with Your everlasting love. Establish my name in blessing, my children in favor, my heritage in glory. May my story become the evidence of a God who loves and a Savior who redeems. Because You have loved me, I can never be cursed. Because You have chosen me, I will forever be blessed.

In Jesus' name, Amen.

DAY 23

BLESSED TO ASCEND

"Who may ascend to Yahweh's hill? Who may stand in his holy place? He who has clean hands and a pure heart, who has not lifted up his soul to falsehood, and who has not sworn deceitfully. He shall receive a blessing from Yahweh, righteousness from the God of his salvation. This is the generation of those who seek Him, who seek your face—even Jacob. Selah."
—Psalms 24:3–6 WEB

Holy and Righteous Father, You are the King of Glory who dwells in holiness. I come before You, washed in the blood of Jesus, purified from sin and cleansed from iniquity. By Your mercy, I ascend the hill of the Lord, and I take my place in Your holy presence. Let every gate of opposition shut before me, and let the blessing reserved for those who seek Your face rest upon me and my household.

Lord, I renounce deceit, idolatry, and compromise. Every unclean altar that seeks to defile my hands is consumed by Your fire. Every impure assignment aimed to corrupt my heart is destroyed by the sword of the Spirit. I declare that I stand clothed in righteousness, equipped to receive the blessing of the Lord that enriches and adds no sorrow.

Father, let generational blessing be my portion. Let my children and my lineage be known as seekers of Your face, carriers of righteousness, and inheritors of divine favor. The blessing of ascending into Your presence shall overshadow the curse of descending into destruction.

Establish me, O God, as a generation set apart—marked by purity, walking in blessing, shining as a city on a hill. From Your holy mountain, release favor, strength, and abundance that no adversary can withstand. My life shall proclaim that those who seek the Lord never walk in shame.

In Jesus' name, Amen.

DAY 24

OUTPOURED BLESSINGS LIKE RAIN

"For I will pour water on him who is thirsty, and streams
on the dry ground. I will pour my Spirit on your
descendants, and my blessing on your offspring; and they
will spring up among the grass, as willows by the
watercourses."
—Isaiah 44:3–4 WEB

O Fountain of Living Waters, I lift my voice to receive the rain of
blessing that flows from Your throne. Let every dry ground in my
life, my family, and my generations be saturated with the streams of
Your Spirit. Lord, pour out upon me abundance that cannot be
contained, joy that cannot be silenced, and prosperity that cannot
be hindered.

Father, I decree that dryness shall no longer be my portion. Every
wilderness is transformed into a watered garden. Every barren
place in my life springs forth with fruitfulness. Let the outpouring
of Your Spirit cover my descendants, making them mighty in the
land, carriers of divine wisdom, and vessels of supernatural
blessing.

By the authority of Christ, I reject the enemy's agenda of famine,
spiritual drought, and unfruitfulness. I decree that my household
shall never lack supply. We are planted by the streams of God and
flourish like willows by the riverside. Let the blessing flow from

generation to generation, increasing in measure and multiplying in glory.

O Lord, cause me and my family to be living testimonies of abundance. Let nations see the evidence of Your rain upon us. Where others wither, we thrive. Where others fail, we flourish. The Spirit of the Lord rests upon us, and His blessing flows without ceasing.

In Jesus' name, Amen.

DAY 25

BLESSING OF PEACE AND PROSPERITY

"But now I will not be to the remnant of this people as in the former days," says Yahweh of Armies. "For the seed of peace and the vine will yield its fruit, and the ground will give its increase, and the heavens will give their dew; and I will cause the remnant of this people to inherit all these things. It shall come to pass that, as you were a curse among the nations, house of Judah and house of Israel, so I will save you, and you shall be a blessing. Don't be afraid. Let your hands be strong."
—Zechariah 8:11–15 WEB

Lord of Hosts, Covenant Keeper, I exalt You as the God who turns seasons and brings restoration. You declare a new day, a new blessing, and a new inheritance for me and my family. No longer shall we be known for curse or shame, but for blessing, peace, and prosperity. You have reversed the former days and appointed a fresh beginning.

I decree that the seed of peace is planted in my life. My vine yields its fruit, my ground increases, and the heavens release their dew upon me. Every power of famine, frustration, and setback is broken. Where there was lack, there is now overflow. Where there was barrenness, there is now fruitfulness.

Father, let every word of curse spoken against my household be silenced forever. We shall not be known for defeat but for victory. We shall not be remembered for struggle but for strength. By Your hand, we are saved, and by Your covenant, we are blessed to be a blessing.

Lord, strengthen my hands to labor and prosper. Establish me as a blessing among the nations. Let every eye see the goodness of the Lord in my life. From this day forward, I walk in the overflow of divine inheritance.

In Jesus' name, Amen.

DAY 26

SEED YET IN THE BARN

"Is the seed yet in the barn? Yes, the vine, the fig tree, the pomegranate, and the olive tree have not produced. From today I will bless you."
—Haggai 2:19 WEB

Faithful Father, today I stand under the decree of blessing You have spoken. Though the seed may yet be hidden, though the vine and the fig tree may not have borne fruit, Your voice has declared, "From today I will bless you." I embrace that prophetic word over my life, my family, and my generations.

Lord, every dormant seed in my life receives divine activation. Every delayed harvest is released by fire. Every power of stagnation, withholding, and barrenness is broken now in the name of Jesus. What seemed fruitless shall flourish, what looked barren shall blossom, and what appeared impossible shall manifest in blessing.

I decree that my vine yields fruit, my fig tree bears increase, my olive tree pours out oil, and my pomegranate overflows with sweetness. The enemies of my harvest are destroyed, and the hands of the wicked are cut off from my inheritance. Today marks a turning point into blessing, favor, and overflow.

Lord, establish me in a covenant of continual blessing. From this day, let abundance speak in my household. From this day, let prosperity be my testimony. From this day, let fruitfulness abound in every area of my life. Your word has gone forth, and it cannot return void.

In Jesus' name, Amen.

DAY 27

DIVINE FAVOR UNSTOPPABLE

"For the Lord God is a sun and shield; the Lord will give grace and glory; no good thing will he withhold from those who walk uprightly."
—Psalm 84:11 WEB

Almighty God, Sovereign Lord, my Sun and my Shield, I declare that Your grace and glory are upon me today. You withhold no good thing from those who seek righteousness, and I position myself under Your covenant favor. Every scheme of the enemy to steal, kill, or destroy my destiny is rendered powerless because Your light surrounds me. I walk uprightly before You, and I decree that Your goodness overtakes every area of my life.

Father, let Your favor shine upon my home, my family, and my work. Let Your shield defend us from spiritual attacks, curses, and manipulations of the enemy. Every attempt to diminish my joy, stall my increase, or hinder my inheritance is shattered by the glory of Your presence. I decree open doors of opportunity, divine protection, and supernatural increase that no adversary can close.

Lord, bless me indeed beyond ordinary measure. Let grace flow like a river into every corner of my life. May the glory of Your Spirit rest upon me and my household, bringing honor, promotion, and provision. I claim every blessing that has been promised to the faithful in Your Word, and I walk boldly in its manifestation.

O God, let my life shine as a testament to Your unwavering goodness. Let every enemy fall silent as the evidence of Your blessing becomes visible. Establish me in prosperity, favor, and divine protection so that I may glorify Your name in all I do.

In Jesus' name, Amen.

DAY 28

BLESSED TO INHERIT

"Blessed are the poor in spirit, for theirs is the kingdom of heaven. Blessed are those who mourn, for they shall be comforted. Blessed are the meek, for they shall inherit the earth. Blessed are those who hunger and thirst for righteousness, for they shall be satisfied. Blessed are the merciful, for they shall receive mercy. Blessed are the pure in heart, for they shall see God. Blessed are the peacemakers, for they shall be called sons of God. Blessed are those who are persecuted for righteousness' sake, for theirs is the kingdom of heaven."
—Matthew 5:3-12 WEB

O Lord of Heaven, King of Glory, I lift my voice in praise, acknowledging Your covenant blessings upon my life. You have promised comfort for the broken, inheritance for the meek, satisfaction for the hungry and thirsty, and mercy for the merciful. I receive every dimension of Your blessing for myself, my household, and my generations. Let every attack of the enemy designed to steal my joy, my peace, or my inheritance be nullified by Your Word.

Father, I claim the kingdom of heaven as my portion. I walk in humility and righteousness, knowing that Your favor rests upon the pure, the peacemakers, and those who pursue Your will. Let persecution and opposition designed to hinder my progress backfire and turn into promotion and glory. Every hand raised against my blessing is broken; every tongue raised in judgment is silenced.

Lord, satisfy the deepest hunger of my spirit with Your righteousness. Let Your mercy envelop my family, protecting us from evil and preserving us for Your glory. I declare that no spiritual enemy, no plot, and no curse shall prosper against us. Your blessings flow into every aspect of our lives, bringing honor, peace, and abundance.

O God, let our lives shine as a testimony of Your faithfulness. Let every act of evil be turned to evidence of Your goodness, and may we walk in the fullness of Your covenant promises. Our inheritance in Christ is secure, and we embrace it fully.

In Jesus' name, Amen.

DAY 29

OVERFLOWING GENEROSITY

"Give, and it will be given to you; good measure, pressed
down, shaken together, running over, will be given to you.
For with the same measure you measure it will be
measured back to you."
—Luke 6:38 WEB

Lord Almighty, Provider of Heaven and Earth, I declare that Your
windows of blessing are open over my life. I receive the fullness of
Your generosity as I walk in obedience, sowing seeds of
righteousness, kindness, and provision. Let every act of giving
bring a harvest pressed down, shaken together, and running over
into my life. No enemy shall intercept the return of Your favor.

Father, protect my family from the schemes of darkness designed
to hinder increase or steal provision. Let the blessing I release
through generosity come back in supernatural multiplication. Let
abundance, favor, and divine increase flow into every area of our
lives. May the enemies of my blessing fall by confusion as Your
hand moves to protect and prosper us.

Lord, let my life be a channel of Your goodness. Let the overflow
from Your Spirit equip me to bless others, establish ministries, and
strengthen families in need. As I measure generosity toward others,
let heaven respond with exceeding and overflowing favor that
sustains me and multiplies across generations.

Almighty God, I decree that every door of opportunity, every seed sown, and every act of obedience is rewarded by Your supernatural provision. Let our household experience peace, abundance, and divine protection, and let Your goodness be our testimony.

In Jesus' name, Amen.

DAY 30

ABUNDANCE FOR EVERY WORK

"God is able to make all grace abound to you, that you,
always having all sufficiency in everything, may abound to
every good work."
—2 Corinthians 9:8 WEB

Gracious Father, Source of all sufficiency, I come before You with thanksgiving, recognizing that Your grace is more than enough to meet every need. You are able to make all grace abound in my life, and I receive it now in fullness for my family, my work, and my destiny. Every plan of the enemy to withhold provision, favor, or blessing is broken by the power of Your Word.

Lord, let abundance overflow into my household, touching every area of life—finances, relationships, health, and ministry. Let every work I undertake prosper under Your guidance, protected from sabotage and evil designs. I decree that what You provide cannot be diminished by human or spiritual opposition. Every effort, every labor, every project is strengthened by Your grace.

Father, position me as a channel of Your blessing. Let my life be a testimony of sufficiency, favor, and supernatural increase. As I abound in every good work, may my influence expand, my legacy be established, and my family be secured in Your covenant promises. Let darkness flee and let Your glory shine in every corner of my life.

O Lord, bless me indeed, that my life may reflect Your abundance, power, and favor. Let Your hand be upon me, protecting and increasing all that concerns me, so that I may walk in overflow and testify of Your goodness.

In Jesus' name, Amen.

EPILOGUE

As we close this journey through *Bless Me Indeed: Unlocking the Overflow of God's Favor*, I want you to pause and reflect on the God you have been encountering through these pages. Jabez's prayer was simple, yet it unlocked a destiny far greater than his circumstances had promised. Likewise, the prayers you have prayed here are not mere words—they are keys that have begun to release covenant blessings into your life, your family, and your future generations.

The God who hears and answers is the same yesterday, today, and forever. He delights in blessing His children, and His favor is not limited by your past, your weaknesses, or the opposition you have faced. Every declaration you have made, every Scripture you have spoken, is planting seeds that will grow into supernatural increase, divine protection, and unshakable peace. The enemy may try to resist, but remember this: the blessing of the Lord is unstoppable, and what heaven releases cannot be reversed by the schemes of darkness.

Let this not be the end of your journey. Take these prayers beyond the pages of this book. Make them a daily rhythm, a lifestyle of expectancy and bold faith. Continue to call upon the God of Israel with the same confidence that Jabez had—asking for His hand to be with you, for your borders to be enlarged, and for His protection to cover every aspect of your life. Let your faith rise, let your voice rise, and let your life rise into the fullness of God's blessing.

The testimony of Jabez is a blueprint for those who will not settle for ordinary. You are a covenant child, an heir of favor, and a carrier of God's blessing. Your life is meant to shine as a beacon of hope, abundance, and divine overflow in a world that desperately needs to see the reality of God's goodness.

Go forth boldly. Speak the promises. Stand in the blessing. And watch as God's favor overtakes every area of your life. Blessing indeed is yours—claim it, walk in it, and let it flow through you to others.

In Jesus' name, Amen.

Encourage Others with Your Story

If this prayer guide has strengthened your faith, deepened your intercession, or helped you stand in the gap, would you consider leaving a short review on Amazon? Your feedback not only encourages others but also helps more believers discover this resource and join in the prayer movement. Every review—just a few sentences—makes a difference. Thank you for being part of this movement.

MORE FROM PRAYERSCRIPTS

Bless Me Indeed:

Unlocking the Overflow of God's Favor

What if you could activate God's favor in your life today and walk in blessings that surpass your wildest expectations?

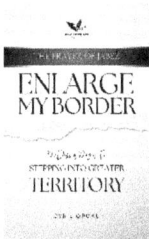

Enlarge My Border:

Stepping Into Greater Territory

Do you feel like you're living beneath your full potential? Do limitations, setbacks, and invisible barriers keep you from stepping into all God has promised? It's time to lift your cry for enlargement.

May Your Hand Be With Me:

Living Under Divine Power and Presence

What happens when the mighty hand of God rests upon your life? Doors open that no man can shut. Strength rises where weakness once prevailed. Guidance comes in the midst of confusion, and protection surrounds you in every battle.

Keep Me From Evil:

Standing Untouchable in Spiritual Warfare

What if the enemy's plans could never touch you or your family? Imagine walking through life completely protected, untouchable, and victorious—no matter what schemes are formed against you.

No More Pain:

Breaking Free from Suffering into Wholeness

Have you been carrying the weight of sorrow, disappointment, or hidden wounds for far too long? Do cycles of pain seem to repeat in your life, your marriage, or your family?

Discern the Enemy:

Sharpening Spiritual Perception to Recognize Satan's Tactics and Guard Your Destiny

The greatest danger is not the enemy you can see—it is the one you cannot. Can you recognize the enemy before he strikes?

Disarm the Enemy:

Stripping Satan of Weapons and Influence Through the Power of Christ

Are you tired of feeling like the enemy has the upper hand in your life? It's time to take back your ground, silence the lies of darkness, and walk in the unstoppable authority of Christ.

Destroy the Enemy:

Breaking Strongholds and Cancelling Evil Works by God's Authority

Are you tired of living under the weight of unseen battles? It's time to rise up and destroy the enemy's works in your life.

Deliver from the Enemy:

Calling on God's Power for Freedom, Rescue, and Lasting Victory

Break free from spiritual attacks and experience God's mighty deliverance in every battle.

Declare Against the Enemy:

Speaking God's Word Boldly to Enforce Triumph Over Darkness

What if you could silence the enemy's schemes, protect your family, and walk boldly into every God-ordained assignment with unshakable authority?

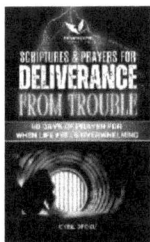

Scriptures & Prayers for Deliverance from Trouble:

40 Days of Prayer for When Life Feels Overwhelming

Are you walking through a season where life feels heavy and your prayers feel weak?

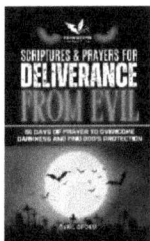

Scriptures & Prayers for Deliverance from Evil:

50 Days of Prayer to Overcome Darkness and Find God's Protection

When darkness presses in, how do you pray?

Scriptures & Prayers for Engaging the Enemy:

70 Days of Prayer to Rebuke the Enemy and Release God's Power

You weren't called to run from the battle—you were anointed to win it.

Scriptures & Prayers for Combating Spiritual Wickedness:

50 Days of Prayer to Overthrow Wicked Plans and Stand in God's Victory

Are you facing opposition that feels deeper than the natural? You're not imagining it—and you're not powerless.

Scriptures & Prayers for Overcoming Through the Blood:

60 Days of Prayers for Claiming Your Blood-Bought Inheritance

You were never meant to fight sin, fear, or Satan in your own strength.

Standing in the Gap for Covenant Awakening:

30 Days of Prayer for National Repentance, Righteous Leadership & God's Sovereign Rule

What if your prayers could help turn the tide of a nation?

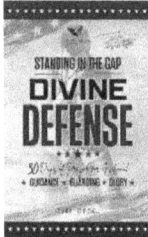

Standing in the Gap for Divine Defense:

30 Days of Prayer for National Guidance, Guarding & Glory

When the foundations of a nation feel as if they're shaking, prayer is the strongest fortress you can build.

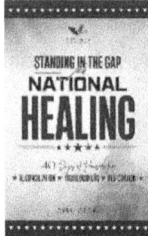

Standing in the Gap for National Healing:

40 Days of Prayer for Reconciliation, Righteousness, and Restoration

What if your prayers could help heal a nation? What if God is waiting for someone—like you—to stand in the gap?

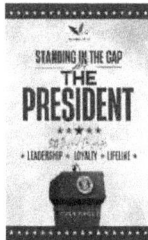

Standing in the Gap for The President:

50 Days of Prayer for Leadership, Loyalty, and Lifeline

When a nation's leader is under spiritual siege, will you answer the call to stand in the gap?

Pardon Through the Blood:

60 Days of Prayers for Total Forgiveness and Freedom

Guilt is a prison. The blood of Jesus holds the key.

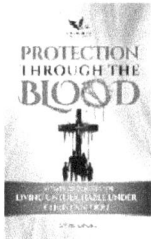

Protection Through the Blood:

60 Days of Prayers for Living Untouchable Under Christ's Blood

You are not helpless. You are not exposed. You are covered— completely—by the blood of Jesus.

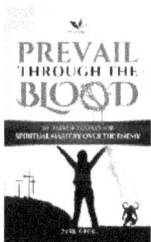

Prevail Through the Blood:

60 Days of Prayers for Spiritual Mastery Over the Enemy

What if every scheme of the enemy against your life could be dismantled—by one unstoppable weapon?

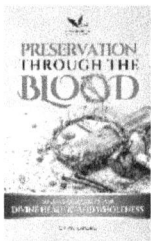

Preservation Through the Blood:

60 Days of Prayers for Divine Healing and Wholeness

Unlock Lasting Healing and Wholeness Through the Blood of Jesus

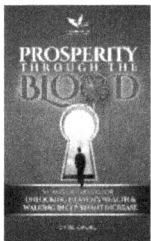

Prosperity Through the Blood:

60 Days of Prayers for Unlocking Heaven's Wealth and Walking in Covenant Increase

You were redeemed for more than survival—you were redeemed to prosper.

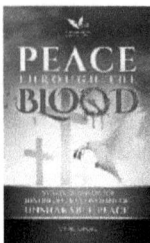

Peace Through the Blood:

60 Days of Prayers for Resting in the Covenant of Unshakable Peace

Are you ready to silence every storm of the mind, heart, and home—once and for all?